BREEDERS' BE

A KENNEL CLUB BO

D0517714

Weimaraner

By Anitra and Roy Cuneo

BREEDERS' BEST®
A KENNEL CLUB BOOK®

WEIMARANER

ISBN: 1-59378-938-6

Copyright © 2004
Kennel Club Books, Inc.
308 Main Street, Allenhurst, NJ 07711 USA
Printed in South Korea

PHOTOS BY:
Paulette Braun,
Bernd Brinkmann,
Isabelle Français,
Carol Ann Johnson and
Mary McGee.

DRAWINGS BY:
Elvira and Yolyanko el Habanero

Contents

CHAPTER 1

Meet the Weimaraner

The name Weimaraner conjures visions of a ghostly image dressed in silver-gray with piercing eyes. Affectionately called the "Gray Ghost" by his admirers, the noble Weimaraner has been revered for centuries as a powerful hunter, noted for his versatile hunting skills and remarkable character. Highly intelligent and affectionate, the Weimaraner has always been known as fearless and protective, prized for his loyalty and devotion to his master.

Historically, the Weimaraner was used for hunting. This most well rounded of breeds is prized for his skills at hunt, point and retrieve.

Although the breed is thought to date back to the 13th century, the first known Weimaraners were developed during the late 1700s by the Grand Duke Karl August of Weimar, Germany to hunt stag, wild boar and wolves. Known as the Weimar Pointer, the breed was prized for its speed, endurance,

The Weimaraner today still exhibits the speed, agility and grace that have won him admirers throughout his history.

courage and exceptional tracking ability. The duke used them as his personal hunting dogs, and he zealously guarded his breeding stock. Only select family members and a few privileged friends were allowed to own his dogs.

That era of protection persisted into the late 1800s, by which time the Weimaraner characteristics had been carefully molded through Duke August's restricted breeding efforts. The breed was further refined later in the 19th century, when it served primarily as a forester's dog, hunting

Along with his myriad talents, the Weimaraner has always been associated with dignity and striking beauty.

large and small game, tracking poachers and defending against predators and ending his work day at home, at his master's feet.

In 1897, the Weimaraner Club of Germany was formed to protect and preserve the breed, with membership restricted to those sportsmen who pledged to retain only their best animals as breeding stock. Three decades later, the Weimaraner Club of Germany and the Austrian Weimaraner Club were launched to maintain the quality of the breed in those countries. Today's Weimaraner is truly an international breed, with breed clubs throughout Europe as well as in the United States, Australia, New Zealand, Canada and South Africa.

The Weimaraner was introduced into the United States in 1929 and officially recognized by the American Kennel Club (AKC) in 1943. During the next decade, the breed experienced a popularity boom, with AKC Weimaraner registrations peaking at over 10,000 in 1957. As an unfortunate consequence, hundreds of inferior-quality Weimaraner pups were bred, bad-tempered and poorly structured animals that were sold to people who were ill-equipped to live with these strong-willed and energetic hunting dogs. Not surprisingly, the popularity curve gradually reversed over the next two decades and by the 1980s breed registration numbers had declined to three or four thousand.

Today's Weimaraner has rebounded, with about 9,000 registered each year, placing the breed in the top 30 most popular AKC breeds. Unfortunately, the number of Weimaraners in animal shelters and rescue groups has increased accordingly, which is one more indication that many new owners remain unpre-

A six-week-old from the breed's homeland, Germany, where breeding has always been closely guarded to ensure quality and consistency.

pared for this curious and exuberant dog. The Weim is adept at hunting fur and feather, equally skilled on upland birds and water fowl. An enthusiastic swimmer, he propels easily through the water with his webbed feet and high head carriage. His tracking ability is well known and admired. Unlike other pointers, he hunts close to the gunner and checks back regularly. Many serious sportsmen "shoot over" Weims and prize them as versatile gundogs.

The Weimaraner also has earned an impressive record in other venues, excelling in conformation, obedience and agility competition. Some also serve as therapy dogs in nursing homes and rehabilitation programs. Weimaraners have worked with search-and-rescue teams to track missing people, and the US government once used them to detect and recover pieces of fired rockets on government missile-testing grounds. Unlike the volatile hunting dog of years ago, today's Weimaraner succeeds at most endeavors for which he was bred.

MEET THE WEIMARANER

Overview

- The Weimaraner's official development dates back to the late 1700s in Weimar, Germany and the Grand Duke Karl August.
- Duke August closely guarded the breed, first known as the Weimar Pointer, by carefully restricting breeding and ownership of his dogs.
- The Weimaraner is an all-around hunting breed with tremendous physical ability and devotion to its master.
- The Weimaraner now has a following worldwide. It has had its ups and downs in the US, but breeders are working diligently to produce the best quality and ability in this multi-talented breed.

Description of the Breed

Pure-bred Weimaraners are not simple accidents of birth. A properly bred Weimaraner is the product of careful breeding, planned according to the breed standard, a written canine "blueprint" of the ideal for the breed, which is the basis of good breeding programs. Without such guidelines, the qualities so valued in the Weimaraner could be diluted or lost completely in successive generations. The United States, United Kingdom and Germany have adopted similar breed standards for the Weimaraner, with the German standard being more detailed and

The breed's eyes are a very distinct feature. The AKC standard lists gray-blue, gray and light amber as acceptable eye colors, and this dashing Weim possesses two out of those three colors.

explicit, emphasizing those qualities it deems most important in the breed.

The Weimaraner is a medium-sized and muscular yet elegant dog, with an aristocratic head and long, lobular ears. The gray coat is short, smooth and sleek. In the US, the Weimaraner usually weighs 70 to 80 pounds, with females a bit smaller than the males. Breed lifespan is 12 to 14 years.

Illustration of Weimaraner body structure.

The Weimaraner's eyes are remarkable. They are light blue at birth. They may change to blue gray, amber or not change at all. If they change, it will be during the first year.

According to the AKC breed standard, a correct Weimaraner male stands 25 to 27 inches tall at the withers, and bitches 23 to 25 inches. The UK and German standards allow dogs and bitches to be one inch shorter than the US version. Germany alone has a weight requirement, with

The glossy gray coat gives the dog a sleek look, emphasizing his musculature.

This handsome Weimaraner and his rightly proud owner have won top honors at many dog shows.

dogs 66 to 88 pounds and bitches 55 to 77 pounds.

The most prominent difference between the American, UK and German standards are in the Weimaraner's temperament and hunting ability. The US version makes no mention at all of hunting skills, stating simply that the dog should present a picture of grace, speed, stamina, alertness and balance. In the UK standard's second paragraph, "Characteristics," there is more emphasis, with "Hunting ability of paramount concern."

The German standard alone specifies "gundog" in the first paragraph, indicating its importance to the German Weimaraner. The fourth paragraph, "Behavior and Character," is even more explicit: "A versatile, easy-going, fearless and enthusiastic gundog with a systematic and persevering search, yet not excessively fast. A remarkably good nose. Sharp on prey and game. Also man-sharp, yet not aggressive. Reliable in pointing and waterwork. Remarkable inclination to work after the shot."

The UK standard is less definitive and most open to interpretation, but it does address temperament, describing it as fearless, friendly, protective, obedient and alert. The American standard omits "protective" from its section on the breed's temperament.

Both the US and UK standards require a docked tail, as the undocked tail is awkward and can be injured when the dog is working in heavy brush. The German standard describes a correct tail but makes no mention that it must be docked.

The German standard is extremely detailed in all other respects. It addresses many more individual body parts, including even the dog's skin. The German "Faults" section lists 16 disqualifying faults and assigns 16 deviations that can be seen as faults. There

The longhaired Weimaraner receives less attention in Europe than the more common shorthaired variety, and little to none in the US. In fact, many

Longhaired Weimaraners follow the same breed standard except for coat length. The coat is seen in the same gray color but is longer all over the body, with feathering on the ears and tail.

is no question that German breeders value the hunting Weimaraner and are dedicated to preserving the breed's original structure and working ability.

American Weim fanciers have never seen the longhaired variety. The mature longhaired coat has a silky texture, is 1 to 2 inches long on the body and can be straight or slightly wavy. Ears and tail are more heavily feathered, and the tail is not docked as in the shorthaired Weim.

The American standard does not recognize the longhaired Weimaraner as a variant of the breed; in fact, the AKC standard states that a "distinctly long coat" is a disqualification. In Europe, the longhaired variety is accepted and occasionally seen at shows. The German standard, which governs most European Weimaraners, goes into great detail in describing the correct coat for a longhaired Weimaraner.

Weimaraner breedings will occasionally produce a shorter, coarser coat type, which is a mixture of the long and shorter coats and called the *Stockhaarig*. When such dogs are registered, the registration number is followed by an "LK" designation to indicate the coat type. In Great Britain, breeders who use the LK dog as breeding stock first must obtain special permission from the British Kennel Club.

DESCRIPTION OF THE BREED

Overview

- The breed standard is a written description of the ideal Weimaraner. This "blueprint" is devised by the parent club to detail the breed's desirable physical conformation as well as correct character and movement.
- Color is very distinct in the breed, with the light eyes creating a dramatic contrast to the sleek silver-gray coat.
- Breed standards in different countries place varied emphasis on temperament and hunting ability, with the German standard being the most specific.
- The less common longhaired Weimaraner is seen occasionally in Europe but very rarely in the US.

Are You a Weimaraner Person?

Thanks to world-famous photographer William Wegman, the Weimaraner has been lauded worldwide and portrayed in books, calendars, greeting cards, magazines and TV commercials. Dressed in costumes and depicted in settings ranging from the silly to the sublime, the Weimaraner is the epitome of a bright and willing participant in the colorful scenarios contrived by photographer/owner Wegman.

Such portraiture can be deceptive, though! Weimaraners are highly intel-

The ever-alert Weim today uses his guarding instincts to provide a watchful eye over his family, home and property.

ligent, very affectionate and devoted to their families, but they are also very energetic, independent-thinking animals who were bred to work and hunt all day. They need training and a variety of high-energy activities to keep them happy and content.

The ideal environment for a Weimaraner is an active family that is willing to spend a lot of time with their dog. This is a true hunting companion, with emphasis on *companion*, who needs the full attention of his person. Despite his hunting ancestry, a Weimaraner is a "people dog" who will not thrive if housed outdoors. Outdoor Weimaraners become lonely and frustrated and often suffer from separation anxiety. They will bark incessantly and develop bad habits and destructive behaviors, a situation that unfortunately often leads to abandonment and possible euthanasia. If you do not want an indoor dog, if you do not want a

Weimaraners are affectionate and versatile dogs that will appreciate the opportunity to accompany their owners whenever possible in whatever activity.

As a hunting/pointing/retrieving breed, the Weimaraner has strong scenting abilities and will be quick to follow his nose if an interesting aroma catches his fancy.

dog that follows you around the house, do *not* allow yourself to get a Weimaraner!

The Weimaraner is neither vicious nor aggresive but is protective of his house and people and will bark at the approach of strangers. His warning bark is deep and intimidating. The Weim will bark indoors as well if he is ignored or left alone too long. His need for human companionship supersedes all else. A neglected Weimaraner will be difficult to housebreak and will attempt to take the upper paw at every opportunity.

The Weimaraner requires lots of exercise, training, time and attention. If these needs are not met, he will become hyperactive and destructive. Puppy class and obedience training are essential to teach him proper rules of behavior and to control his rambunctious nature. He must learn to respect and obey all members of the family, not just one owner/trainer. Weimaraner rescue groups frequently take in dogs from owners who were unprepared for the commitment required for living with this active and demanding breed.

The modern Weimaraner retains his ancestral hunting instinct for small furry animals. While he may learn to tolerate and befriend cats and other dogs, his prey drive will kick in over rabbits, squirrels and pet birds. Such tendencies can seldom be reversed. If you can't deal with the possibility of such behavior, think twice about getting a Weimaraner.

Weimaraner fanciers who want a personal gundog should select their puppy from breeding stock with field experience— parents that are successful hunters or have a pedigree

Training your Weimaraner is absolutely essential. You must establish yourself as boss of this intelligent, strong breed if the two of you are to enjoy a mutually happy relationship.

with titles that prove the ancestors' merit in the field. Weims are not big-running dogs who range far afield from their hunting partners. Most are tractable, easy-handling dogs of moderate range, considered to be good "buddy-type" hunting dogs who hunt close.

Weimaraners belong to the HPR group of dog breeds, gundogs that hunt, point and retrieve, which makes the breed a versatile, all-around gundog. The close working relationship between the Weimaraner

"Gray ghost" times two! Many have been attracted to the breed for its majestic appearance—like no other in dogdom.

and the hunter creates a dependent and protective aura in the dog.

Training methods, however, must be firm but gentle, for despite his stubborn streak, he is also very sensitive. Harsh treatment will make him surly and uncooperative at home and in the field.

Weimaraner owners will tell you that their dogs are worth the effort. These are intelligent and affectionate dogs who will reward your efforts with unconditional love and devotion.

Owners appreciate the Weim's "all-business" bark when it comes to protecting their homes.

ARE YOU A WEIMARANER PERSON?

Overview

- The Weimaraner person is ready and able to establish himself as leader of the intelligent and sensitive Weimaraner.
- The Weimaraner person has time to exercise and care for the dog and can provide ample accommodations both inside and outside the home.
- The Weimaraner person is responsible and available, for this breed is highly devoted and will not be happy unless it can spend most of its time with its owners.
- The Weimaraner person makes certain that his dog is safe at all times, taking into consideration that the breed's hunting instincts may incite it to follow its nose.

CHAPTER 4

Selecting a Breeder

A good breeder is as important as a good Weimaraner pup. You can't get one without the other. Whatever your reason for wanting a Weimaraner... hunting, companionship, dog shows or obedience competition...you want a healthy dog with excellent temperament and correct Weimaraner instincts. Otherwise, why get a Weimaraner?

A puppy search can be an emotionally trying experience, taxing your patience and your willpower. There is no prize for the Weim enthusiast who

The striking eyes and intelligent expression impart the Weim's look of intelligence even in youngsters.

finds a puppy the fastest! Actually, that anxious new owner wins the booby prize! Slow down and do this right. If you rush into your breeder and puppy selection, you may pay the price over and over—at the vet's office in dollars and cents and in your heart and home, where the price cannot be estimated.

Be prepared to lose your heart when you visit a litter of these sweet, adorable gray pups, but you'll need to keep your head to make a wise choice!

All puppies are adorable, and it's easy to fall in love with the first cute pup you see, but a poorly bred Weimaraner will have health and temperament problems that can empty your wallet and break your heart. A responsible breeder is the only source for a healthy pup that is well suited to your lifestyle and long-term goals. Do your breeder homework before you visit litters. Arm yourself with a list of questions for the breeder (a good one will expect that). Then leave your wallet at home so you aren't tempted to cave in. Do not

It's hard work being a mom to a litter of pups who are usually hungry or otherwise clamoring for motherly attention.

rush out right away to find that Weim puppy. Take your time and consider all of the options and factors. Trust what we say here—do it right, and do it once!

For starters, when you're with the breeder, ask to see the litter's pedigrees and registration papers. The pedigree should include three to five generations of ancestry. Ask the breeder to explain any titles in the pedigree. Titles simply indicate a dog's accomplishments in some area of canine competition, which adds to the breeder's credibility and proves the merits of the ancestors. While it is true that a pedigree and registration papers do not guarantee health or good temperament, a well-constructed pedigree is still a good insurance policy.

Ask the breeder why he planned this litter. A good breeder should explain the genetics behind this particular breeding and what he expects the breeding to produce. He never breeds because "his Weimaraner is sweet and/or beautiful, the neighbor's dog is handsome, they will have lovely puppies," and so on. Just loving his dog like mad does not qualify an individual to breed dogs intelligently or properly raise a litter of Weimaraner pups.

Ask the breeder about health clearances. Weimaraners may develop hip and elbow dysplasia or eye disease, and the only way to produce puppies that are not affected is to screen the parents for those defects. Cancer is also a concern for Weim breeders. Ask the breeder if the sire and dam have hip clearances from the OFA (Orthopedic Foundation for Animals, a national canine hip registry). Have the parents' eyes been examined within the past year by a board-certified veterinary

Observe pups and adults alike when you visit the breeder. The quality, health and personality of all Weims on the premises, as well as the cleanliness of their living quarters, tells volumes about the breeder and how much care he puts into breeding and puppy-raising.

ophthalmologist? Eye clearances can be registered with the Canine Eye Registration Foundation (CERF). Good breeders will gladly, in fact proudly, provide those documents. For more information on genetic disease in Weimaraners, you can contact the Weimaraner Club of America (WCA) on the web www.weimclubamerica.org.

The breeder should explain that Weimaraners are prone to a condition called bloat (gastric dilatation/volvulus). This is a life-threatening condition that is common in deep-chested breeds such as the Weimaraner, Bloodhound, Boxer, Great Dane and other similarly constructed breeds. Torsion occurs when the stomach fills rapidly with air and begins to twist, cutting off the blood supply. If not treated immediately, the dog will die. For more information on this condition, check out the WCA website. No one knows for certain what causes bloat, so unfortunately there are no defined preventives.

Experienced Weimaraner breeders are frequently involved in some aspect of the dog fancy with their dog(s), perhaps showing or training them for some type of performance event or other dog-related activity. Their Weim(s) may have earned titles in various canine competitions, which is added proof of their experience and commitment to the breed.

Dedicated breeders who are truly involved with their dogs often belong to the WCA and/or a local breed or kennel club. Such affiliation with other experienced breeders and sportsmen expands their knowledge of the breed and breed characteristics, which further enhances a breeder's credibility. Quality breeders, by the way, do not raise several different breeds of dog or produce multiple litters of pups throughout the year; one or two litters a year is typical.

have owned, which breeds of dog and what became of those dogs. He will want to know your living arrangements, i.e., house, yard, kids, etc., your goals for this pup and how you plan to raise him. The breeder's

What does the breeder do with her dogs? Show, hunt, compete in performance events? A good breeder will be involved in some aspect of the fancy and be a member of a recognized breed club.

Responsible breeders will ask *you* questions, too... about your dog history, previous dogs you

primary concern is the future of his puppies and whether you and your family are suitable owners who will provide a proper and loving home for his precious little one. Avoid any breeder who agrees to sell you a Weimaraner puppy "no questions asked." Such indifference indicates a lack of concern about the pups and casts doubt on the breeder's ethics and his breeding program.

A reputable breeder will also warn you about the downside of the Weimaraner. No breed of dog is perfect, nor is every breed suitable for every person's temperament and lifestyle. Be prepared to weigh the good news with the bad about the Weim. Remember that this is a solid, powerful dog who thrives on activity and attention.

Most reputable breeders have a puppy sales contract that includes specific health guarantees and reasonable return policies. The breeder should agree to accept a

puppy back if things do not work out. He also should be willing, indeed anxious, to check up on the puppy's progress after it leaves home and be available if you have questions or problems with the pup.

Many breeders place their pet-quality puppies on what is called the AKC's Limited Registration. This does register the pup with the AKC, but it does not allow the registration of any offspring from that dog. The purpose of a limited registration is to prevent indiscriminate breeding of "pet-quality" Weimaraners. The breeder, and only the breeder, can cancel this limited registration if the adult dog develops into breeding quality.

If you have any doubts at all, feel free to ask for references…and check them out. It's unlikely that a breeder will offer names of unhappy puppy clients, but any bit of information you can glean will make you more comfortable dealing with a particular breeder.

You can expect to pay a dear price for all of these bargain Weim is not a bargain at all. Indeed, the discount pup is in reality a potential disaster that has little chance of developing into a healthy, stable adult.

Three adolescents growing up strong. Breeders put health first when planning a mating, making sure that the parents are free of genetic defects, including orthopedic problems.

breeder qualities, whether you fancy a pet-quality Weimaraner for a companion dog or one with show, field or competition potential. The discount or Such "bargains" could ultimately cost you a fortune in vet expenses and heartache that can't be measured in dollars and cents.

So how does one find a responsible breeder who meets all of the aforementioned qualifications? Do your puppy homework! Spend several days at dog shows or other dog events where you can meet breeders and exhibitors and get to know their dogs. Most Weimaraner fanciers are more than happy to show off their dogs and brag about their accomplishments. If you know a Weimaraner you are fond of, ask the owner where he got his dog. Check with the AKC for breeder referrals in your area. Their website (www. akc.org) as well as that of the WCA offers links to breed clubs and breeders throughout the US.

Where *not* to look for your Weimaraner puppy? Don't read the newspaper! Reputable breeders rarely advertise in newspapers. They are very particular about prospective puppy owners and do not rely on mass advertising to attract the right people. Rather, they depend on referrals from other breeders and previous puppy clients. They are more than willing to keep any puppy past the usual eight-week placement age until the right person comes along.

Puppy brokers, that is, backyard breeders who breed more than a single breed, are the worst possible sources of quality pups of any breed. These are for-profit operations

Here's Ollie on his way to his championship! Bred by Michael and Amy Anderson, Ch. GraytSky's Heart of Dixie is proudly owned by Suzanne and Anthony Restivo.

that care only about the bottom-line dollar and not about the health or stability of the puppies they mass-produce. A newspaper ad will likely lead you right to one of these dismal operations. Even if you "just want a nice pet," you still want a healthy pup with a good disposition. A good breeder is your only choice. It should be pointed out here that some good breeders do breed two breeds at the same time. Don't be put off if the kennel has Weims and Golden or Labrador Retrievers, but if they are breeding six sporting breeds, three terrier breeds and the ugliest toys you've ever seen—run, run, run!

Aside from thorough research, perhaps the second most important ingredient in your breeder search is patience. You will not likely find the right breeder or litter on your first go-around. Breeders often have waiting lists, but a good pup is worth the wait.

SELECTING A BREEDER

Overview

- Contact the American Kennel Club or the Weimaraner Club of America by mail, phone or email. These clubs can point you toward a reputable breeder.
- Visit dog shows to meet breeders and handlers of good dogs.
- Know what to expect from a quality breeder and don't rush into things.
- Be patient! The good breeder will happily share pedigrees, sales agreements, health clearances, registration papers and references with you.
- The breeder should inform you about the incidence of hip and elbow dysplasia, cancer, eye disease and other conditions in his line.

Finding the Right Puppy

S electing the right puppy is part two of your Weimaraner breeder-puppy search. The perfect pup is seldom right around the corner. Visit several litters if possible and keep notes on what you like…and don't like…about each one. You may have to travel to visit a good litter, but your research will pay off. Up close and personal is the only way to choose your pup. That way you can become better acquainted with

At six weeks of age, this pup is ready for visits from prospective owners, but it will still be a few weeks before he can leave for his new home.

the breeder, the mother of the pups and the environment in which the pups are being raised.

Visiting a litter involves much more than puppy hugs and kisses. It's more like your ultimate job interview. While searching for your new Weimaraner family member, you'll be checking out the applicants...the puppies, their parents, the breeder and of course the area in which the pups are kept.

The breeder identifies the pups by putting different-colored ribbons around their necks at this early age.

Where and how a litter of pups is raised are vitally important to the pups' early development into confident and friendly Weimaraners. Weimaraner puppies need to be socialized daily with people and people activities. The litter should be kept indoors, in the house or in an adjoining sheltered area, not isolated in a basement, garage or outside kennel building. The greater the pups' exposure to household sights and sounds between three to four

Two generations of beauty, health and soundness. The object of any reputable breeder is to pass on only the best traits of the breed with every mating.

weeks and seven weeks of age, the easier their adjustment will be to their human family.

When you visit a litter, scrutinize the puppies as well as their living area for cleanliness as well as signs of sickness or poor health. The pups should be reasonably clean (allowing for normal non-stop "puppy-pies"). They should appear energetic, bright-eyed and alert. Healthy pups have clean, thick coats, are well proportioned and feel solid and muscular without being overly fat and pot-bellied. Watch for crusted eyes or noses and any watery discharge from the noses, eyes or ears. Check for evidence of watery or bloody stools.

Visit with the dam and the sire if possible. In many cases the sire is not on the premises, but the breeder should have photos and a resume of his characteristics and accomplishments. Pay special attention to the personality of the parents. Weimaraners can be somewhat aloof with strangers but should not shy away from a friendly overture. It is also normal for some dams to be somewhat protective of their young, but overly aggressive behavior is unacceptable. Puppies can learn behavior from the parents, and if one or both parents are aggressive or very shy, it is likely that some of the pups will behave similarly.

Notice how the pups interact with their littermates and their surroundings, especially their responses to people. They should be active, friendly and outgoing, not shy or spooky at every sight or sound. In most Weimaraner litters, some pups will be more outgoing than others, but even a quiet pup that is properly socialized should not shrink from a friendly voice or outstretched hand.

The breeder should be honest in discussing any differences in puppy personalities. Although many breeders do some sort of Weimaraner puppy that is right for you and your lifestyle.

Tell the breeder whether you plan to show your pup in conformation or compete in other types of competition or

Early life lessons come from whom else but Mom?

temperament testing, they also spend the first eight weeks of the pups' lives cuddling them and cleaning up after them. Thus they get to know very well the subtle differences in each pup's personality. The breeder's observations are valuable aids in selecting a Weimaraner-related activities. Some pups will show more promise than others, and he can help you select one that will best suit your long-term goals.

Do you prefer a male or a female? Which one is right for you? Both sexes are loving and loyal, and any differences are due more to individual personalities than to sex. The Weimaraner female is a gentle soul and easy to live with. She also can be a bit more moody, depending on her whims and hormonal peaks.

The male is often up to two inches taller than the female and overall bigger and more powerful. Although males tend to be more even-tempered than bitches, they are also more

Your decision to add a Weimaraner to your life means the start of an exciting and rewarding friendship with a bright, talented and personable canine companion.

physical and exuberant during adolescence, which can be problematic in a large and powerful dog. An untrained male also can become dominant with people and other dogs. A solid foundation in obedience is necessary if you want the dog to respect you as his leader.

Intact males tend to be more territorial, especially with other male dogs. In male puppies, both testicles should be descended into the scrotum. A dog with undescended testicles will make a fine pet but will be ineligible to compete in the show ring.

By seven weeks of age, the pups should have had at least one worming and their first puppy shots, and have certificates from the vet that verify their good health at the time of the exam. Some Weimaraner breeders feel that separating the vaccines in a puppy's booster shots into single-vaccine injections reduces the possibility of negative reactions to the various components in the combination vaccines. Ask your breeder and your veterinarian for their recommendations.

The breeder should tell you what the pups have been eating, when and how much. Some send home a small supply of puppy food to mix with your own for the first few days. Most breeders give their clients a puppy "take-home packet," which includes a copy of the health certificate, the puppy's pedigree and registration papers, copies of the parents' health clearances and the breeder's sales contract if he has one. Any reputable breeder will give you time to take the pup to your vet in order to confirm that the puppy does not have any discernible congenital defects. If you are not happy with the vet's findings, the breeder should accept the puppy back and refund your money. Discuss this before you purchase the pup.

FINDING THE RIGHT PUPPY

Overview

- Visit the litter to see the puppies firsthand. You are seeking healthy, sound puppies. It's wise to visit the litter a second time to be sure the pup you've selected is still the one you like the best.
- Make a wise choice. Don't just fall for the first pup you see!
- Trust that your breeder knows the pups well and can guide you to a puppy that fits your lifestyle and personality.
- Do you want a male or a female puppy? Consider the few sex-related personality and physical differences.
- If you intend to show or compete, discuss this with the breeder.

Welcoming the Weimaraner

Your puppy homework isn't finished yet. You need to stock up on puppy supplies and prepare the house before your pup comes home. A thorough puppy-proofing will prevent any accidents or surprises that could be dangerous and even fatal for your pup. It also will preserve your property and your peace of mind.

Puppy shopping is the fun part, but hang on to your purse strings. Puppy stuff, especially the non-essentials, is often too cute to resist, so "stocking up" can easily decimate your budget. Start with basic essentials and save the puppy goodies until later.

Your pup is used to snuggling up with his littermates each day, and this is what he will miss most when he first comes home. Be sure to give him a warm and affectionate welcome to help him adjust.

PUPPY FOOD

Your Weimaraner pup should be fed a quality food that is appropriate for his age and breed. Most quality dog foods now offer specific formulas that address the nutritional needs of small, medium and large breeds of dog during the various stages of their lives. Be prepared with a good growth food, which should be his diet for his first year. After that you can switch to a quality adult-maintenance food.

The active Weimaraner loves to have a safely enclosed yard in which to run and play. You must puppy-proof your home both inside and out.

Your Weimaraner's early growth period as well as his long-term health will benefit from a diet of high-quality puppy and adult dog food. Canine nutrition is addressed in greater detail in the chapter on proper feeding regimens. For experienced recommendations, check with your breeder and your vet before you buy your puppy's food.

A fun fuzzy toy should help your puppy settle in and feel right at home.

DINNERWARE

You'll need two separate serving bowls, one for food and one for water. Stainless steel pans are your best choices, as they are chew-proof and easy to clean. Tip-proof is a good idea, since most puppies love to splash about in their water bowls, and the Weimaraner is no exception.

grows. Lightweight nylon adjustable collars work best for both pups and adult dogs. Put the collar on as soon as the pup comes home so he can get used to wearing it. The ID tag should have your phone number, name and address, but *not* the puppy's name, as that would enable a stranger to identify and call your dog.

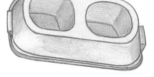
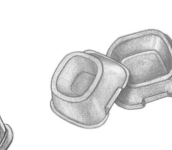

Purchase food and water bowls that are durable, chew-proof and easy to clean.

COLLARS AND ID TAGS

Your Weimaraner pup should have an adjustable collar that expands to fit him as he

Some owners include a line that says "Dog needs medication" to speed the dog's return if he is lost or stolen. Attach the tag with an "O" ring (the kind used in key rings) rather than an "S" link, as the latter can snag carpets and snap off.

Today even dog collars have gone high tech. Some come equipped with beepers and tracking devices. The most advanced pet identification tool uses a Global Positioning System and fits inside a collar or tag. When your dog leaves his programed home perimeter, the device sends a message directly to your phone or email address.

Use a well-made conventional leather or nylon collar on your Weimaraner. This collar can also be used during lessons. Training collars should never be used on Weimaraner puppies under 16 weeks of age.

LEASHES

For puppy's safety and your own convenience, his leash wardrobe should include at least two kinds of leads. A narrow six-foot leather leash is best for walks, puppy kindergarten, obedience class and training to heel. A flexible lead is extendable and housed in a large handle. It extends and retracts with the push of a button. A flexible lead is the ideal tool for exercising puppies and adult dogs but is not recommended for beginners. It is available in several lengths (8 feet to 26 feet) and strengths, depending on breed size. Longer is better, as it allows your dog to run about and check out the good sniffing areas farther away from you. Flexible leads are especially handy for exercising your puppy in unfenced areas or when traveling with your dog.

The flexible lead extends to give the dog more freedom to explore and retracts when you want to keep him in close.

CHAPTER 6

BEDDING

Dog beds are just plain fun. Beds run the gamut from small and inexpensive to elegant, high-end beds suitable for the most royal of dog breeds. However, don't go crazy just yet. Better to save that fancy bed for when your Weimaraner is older and less likely to shred it up or make a puddle in it. For puppy bedding, it's best to use a large towel, mat or blanket that can be easily laundered (which will probably be often).

CRATING AND GATING

These will be your most important puppy purchases. A crate is your most valuable tool for housebreaking your pup, and his favorite place to feel secure. Crates come in three varieties, wire mesh, fabric mesh and the familiar airline-type plastic crate. Wire or fabric crates offer the best ventilation and some conveniently fold up suitcase-style. Whatever your choice, purchase an adult-size crate, about 22 inches wide by 36 inches high, rather than a small or puppy size; your Weim will soon grow into it. Crates are available at most pet stores. We recommend using carpet in the rear part of the crate and newspaper in the front part until the puppy is housebroken. Feed the pup on the carpet.

A well-placed baby gate will protect your puppy while safeguarding your house from the inevitable puppy mischief. It is wise to confine puppy to a tiled or uncarpeted room or space, one that is accessible to the outside door he will use

You must buy a crate for your Weimaraner puppy, but get one from the outset that will house the full-grown dog. Wire crates are the best choice for use in the home, as they provide safe confinement while allowing the dog to feel part of his surroundings.

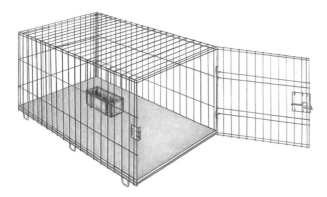

40

for potty trips. Gated to a safe area where he cannot wreak havoc or destruction, puppy will soon master house-breaking, chew only appropriate chew toys rather than your antique furniture and save himself from unnecessary corrections for normal puppy mishaps.

Gated, however, does not mean unsupervised. Weimaraners get bored easily and have been known to chew through doors and drywall. If puppy must be unattended, use his crate.

GROOMING TOOLS

Weimaraners are easy keepers. You don't need a battery of combs and brushes to keep them tidy. A grooming glove and damp washcloth are the only implements needed to maintain a clean and shiny coat. Introduce your puppy to grooming early on so he learns to like it. Start with a soft bristle brush at this tender age. Brushing also helps condition the pup to hands-on attention, which will be invaluable when you have to clean his teeth and ears and clip his nails.

HOME SAFETY

Along with shopping for puppy accessories, you must puppy-proof your house before the pup comes home. Weimaraner pups are naturally curious critters that will investigate everything new, then seek-and-destroy just because it's fun. The message here is: never let your puppy roam your house unsupervised. Scout your house for the following hazards:

Trash cans and diaper pails are natural puppy magnets (hey, they know where the good stuff is!).

Medication bottles, cleaning materials and roach and rodent poisons and insect repellents must be kept from your Weim's great nose! Lock these up. You'll be amazed at what a determined puppy can find.

Unplug all electrical cords wherever you can and make them inaccessible. Injuries from chewed electrical cords are extremely common in young dogs. Use plastic disks in all wall sockets.

Dental floss, yarn, needles and thread and other stringy stuff are puppy favorites! Puppies snuffling about at ground level will find and ingest the tiniest of objects and will end up in surgery. Most vets will gladly tell you stories about the stuff they have surgically removed from puppies' stomachs.

Discard any toilet-bowl cleaners, as these can be toxic for your dog. All dogs are born with toilet sonar and quickly discover that the water there is always cold.

Beware of tools and chemicals in your garage or shed! Antifreeze is expecially dangerous. It has a sweet taste attractive to animals but is extremely toxic. Just a few drops will kill an adult Weimaraner, even less for a puppy. Lock it up well out of reach.

Socks, underwear, shoes, slippers and the like must be put in the proper places. Keep them off the floor and close your closet doors. Puppies love all of the above because they smell like their favorite person—you!

SOCIALIZATION

This actually puppy-proofs your puppy, not your house. Puppy socialization is your Weimaraner's insurance policy to a happy, stable adulthood. It is the most important element in a Weimaraner puppy's introduction to the human world. Weimaraners are by nature one-family dogs that are very selective of the people they choose to like and trust. Thus it is most important to expose them to strangers and new situations at an early age. Canine research has proven that unsocialized pups, especially those with protective instincts like Weimaraners, grow up to have unfortunately they are ultimately euthanized. Puppy socialization lays the foundation for a well-behaved adult

Kids love dogs, and the feeling will be mutual if the introductions are supervised and the children are taught how to handle a dog with care and respect.

temperament problems. They may be fearful of people, children and strange places. Some may turn into fear-biters or become aggressive with other dogs, strangers, even family members. Such dogs can seldom be rehabilitated and often end up abandoned in animal shelters where canine, thus preventing those canine behaviors that lead to the sad situation of abandonment and eventual euthanasia.

The primary socialization period occurs during a puppy's first 20 weeks of life. Once he leaves the safety of his mom and littermates at seven to ten weeks of age, your job begins. Start with a quiet, uncomplicated household for the first day or two, then gradually introduce him to the sights and sounds of his new human world. Christmas is never a good time for a puppy to enter his new home.

Frequent interaction with children, new people and other dogs is essential at this age. Visit new places (dog-friendly, of course) like parks or even the local grocery store parking lot where there are crowds of people. Set a goal of two new places a week for the next two months. Keep these new situations upbeat and positive, which will create a positive attitude toward future encounters. Be friendly and casual when meeting people; your puppy will adopt your attitude.

"Positive" is especially important when visiting your veterinarian. You don't want a pup that quakes with fear every time he sets a paw inside his doctor's office. Make sure your vet is a true dog lover as well as a dog doctor.

Your puppy also will need supervised exposure to children. Weimaraners are generally good with young-sters, but both dog and child must learn how to behave properly with each other. Puppies of all breeds tend to view little people, such as children, as littermates, and will attempt to exert the upper paw (a dominance ploy) over the child. Weimaraners are headstrong dogs who could unintentionally hurt a child in play. They also have inquiring minds and do not take well to simple and repetitive children's games. Children must learn how to properly play with the dog and to respect his privacy. Likewise, adult family members should supervise and teach the puppy not to nip or jump up on the kids.

Take your Weimaraner youngster to puppy school.

Some classes accept pups from 10 to 12 weeks of age, with one series of puppy shots as a health requirement. The younger the pup, the easier it is to shape good behavior patterns. A good puppy class teaches proper canine social etiquette rather than rigid obedience skills. Your puppy will meet and play with young dogs of other breeds, and you will learn about the positive teaching tools you'll need to train your pup. Puppy class is important for both novice and experienced puppy folks. If you're a smart Weimaraner owner, you won't stop there and will continue on with a basic obedience class. Of course, you want the best-behaved Weimaraner in the neighborhood.

Remember this: there is a direct correlation between the quality and amount of time you spend with your puppy during his first 20 weeks of life and the character of the adult dog he will become. You cannot recapture this valuable learning period, so make the most of it.

WELCOMING THE WEIMARANER

Overview

- Go to the pet store before puppy comes home. You will need the essentials, including food, bowls, a collar and ID tags, toys, a leash, a crate, some basic grooming tools and more.
- Make your home safe for your puppy by removing dangers from the dog's environment indoors and out.
- Socialization is critical to your puppy's proper development. Be proactive by introducing him to children and other dogs, along with new experiences, keeping it positive and fun.
- Try a puppy class as a way to socialize and train your new pup.

Your Puppy's Education

If you want to live in harmony with your Weimaraner, you have to be the top dog in his life. The Weim is a strong and powerful dog that is famous for his stubborn streak, so early training is especially important for a Weimaraner. Puppy kindergarten should start the day you bring your puppy home.

Before your puppy left his breeder, all of his life lessons came from his mom and littermates. When he played too rough or nipped too hard, his siblings cried and stopped the game. When he got pushy or obnoxious, his mother cuffed him gently with a

The first step on the road to a well-behaved dog is beginning your puppy's lessons at an early age, when he is eager to soak up everything you can teach him.

maternal paw. Now his human family has to communicate appropriate behavior in terms his little canine mind will understand. Remember, too, that from a canine perspective human rules make no sense at all.

When you start the teaching process, keep this thought uppermost: the first 20 weeks of any canine's life are the most valuable learning time, a period when his mind is best able to soak up every lesson, both positive and negative. Positive experiences and proper socialization during this period are critical to his future development and stability. We'll learn more about socialization later, but know this: the amount and quality of time you invest with your Weim youngster now will determine what kind of an adult he will become. Wild dog—or gentleman or lady? Well-behaved or naughty dog? It's up to you.

Canine research tells us that any

From your Weim's first sit to his perfect performance in the obedience ring, you will be a proud, rewarded owner.

Be firm and fair when training your Weimaraner. No dog likes to be scolded; positive reinforcement, with occasional corrections only when necessary, is the best way to get results.

behavior that is rewarded will be repeated (this is called positive reinforcement). If something good happens, like a tasty treat or hugs and kisses, puppy will naturally want to repeat the behavior. Canine behavioral science also has proven that one of the best ways to a puppy's mind is through his stomach. Never underestimate the power of liver!

This leads to a very important puppy rule: keep your pockets loaded with puppy treats at all times so you are prepared to reinforce good behavior whenever it occurs. The same "reward-him-if-he's-good" reinforcement principle also applies to negative behavior, or what we humans might consider negative (like digging in the trash can, which the dog or puppy does not know is "wrong"). If pup gets into the garbage, steals food or does anything else that makes him feel good, he will do it

again. What better reason to keep a sharp eye on your puppy to prevent those "normal" canine behaviors?

You are about to begin Puppy Class 101. Rule number one: puppy must learn that you are now the "alpha" dog and his new pack leader. Rule number two: you have to teach him in a manner he will understand (sorry, barking just won't do it). Remember always that the pup knows nothing about human standards of behavior.

WORD ASSOCIATION
Use the same word (command) for each behavior every time you teach it, adding food rewards and verbal praise to reinforce the positive behavior. Pup will make the connection and will be motivated to repeat the action when he hears those key words. For example, when teaching pup to potty outside, use the same potty term ("Go potty," "Get busy" or "Hurry

up" are commonly used) each time he eliminates, adding a "Good boy!" while he's urinating or emptying his bowels. Pup will soon learn what those trips outside are for.

PUPPY-TRAINING PRINCIPLES

All dogs learn their lessons in the present tense. You have to catch them in the act (good or bad) in order to dispense rewards or discipline. You have three to five seconds to connect with your dog or he will not understand what he did wrong. Thus timing and consistency are your keys to success in teaching any new behavior or correcting any bad behavior.

Successful puppy training depends on several important principles:

1. Use simple one-word commands and say them only once. Otherwise, puppy learns that "Come" (or "Sit" or "Down") is a three- or four-word command.

2. Never correct your dog for something he did minutes earlier. You have three to

For your dog's safety, he must reliably come to you when called. You can begin teaching this command to youngsters in the form of a game.

five seconds to catch him. Be on your toes—puppies commit crimes quickly.

3. Always praise (and offer a treat) as soon as he does something good (or stops doing something naughty). How else will puppy know he's a good dog?

4. Be consistent. You can't snuggle together on the couch to watch TV today, then scold him for climbing

onto the couch tomorrow.

5. Never tell your dog to come and then correct him for something he did wrong. He will think the correction is for coming to you. (Think like a dog, remember?) Always go to the dog to stop unwanted behavior, but be sure you catch him in the act.

6. Never hit or kick your dog or strike him with a newspaper or other object. Such physical abuse will only create fear and confusion in your dog and could provoke aggressive behavior down the road.

7. When praising or correcting, use your best doggie voice. Use a light and happy voice for praise and a firm, sharp voice for warnings or corrections. A whiny "No, No" or "Drop that" will not sound too convincing, nor will a deep, gruff voice make your puppy feel like he's been a good fellow.

Your dog also will respond accordingly to family arguments. If there's a shouting match, he will think that he did something wrong and head for cover. So never argue in front of the kids…or the dog!

Despite the Weimaraner's powerful appearance, he is a soft dog who will not respond to harsh training methods or corrections. Puppy kindergarten and continued lessons in obedience are the best course to combating the Weim's stubborn streak.

GAMES WITH YOUR PUPPY
Puppy games are a great way to entertain your puppy and yourself, while subliminally teaching lessons in the course of having fun. Start with a game plan and a pocketful of tasty dog treats. Keep your games short so you don't push his attention span beyond Weimaraner puppy limits. Weims get bored with too much repetition.

"Puppy catch-me" is a game that helps to teach the come

command. With two people sitting on the floor about 10 or 15 feet apart, one person holds and pets the pup while the other calls him, "Puppy, puppy, come!" in a happy voice. When your puppy comes running, lavish him with big hugs and

and toss it back and forth for puppy to retrieve. When he picks it up, praise and hug some more, give him a goodie to release the toy, then toss it back to person number two. Repeat as above.

Hide-and-seek also teaches

When you begin teaching commands, your first exercise will likely be the sit, as this is usually the easiest for dogs to master.

give him a tasty treat. Repeat back and forth several times, but don't overdo it. The "heel" and "come" commands should be given only on-leash until the dog understands the commands.

You can add a ball or toy

the pup to "come." Play this game outdoors in your yard or other confined safe area. When pup is distracted, hide behind a tree. Peek out to see when he discovers you are gone and comes running back to find you (trust us, he will do that). As soon as he gets close, come out, squat down with arms outstretched and call him, "Puppy, come!" This is also an excellent bonding aid and teaches puppy to depend on you.

"Where's your toy?" is an ideal beginner retrieving game. Begin by placing one of his favorite toys in plain sight, ask your puppy "Where's your toy?" and let him take it. Then place your puppy safely outside the room and place the toy where only part of it shows. Bring him back and ask the same question. Praise highly when he finds it. Repeat several times. Finally, conceal the toy completely and let your puppy sniff it out. Trust his nose…he will find his toy.

Weim puppies love to have fun with their people. Games are excellent teaching aids and one of the best ways to say "I love you" to your puppy.

Visit your pet shop for fun, safe, interactive toys.

Down is another of the basic commands. It is a bit more difficult to accomplish but, once learned, you will find the down and down/stay to be very useful commands.

YOUR PUPPY'S EDUCATION

Overview

- The first 20 weeks are your puppy's most critical learning time. Take advantage and teach him right away.
- Using treats and positive reinforcement is the best way to train any dog, especially one as sensitive as the Weimaraner.
- Know the basic rules of puppy classes: you are "alpha," and you have to learn to speak "dog."
- Teach word association, timing and consistency.
- Learn the basic principles of successful puppy training.
- Play games with your puppy to help him learn to come when called.

WEIMARANER

House-training Your Weimaraner

very Weimaraner puppy deserves a room of his own, a cozy and safe harbor where he can feel secure. I know what you're thinking…and, no, a crate is neither cruel nor is it punishment for your pup. Canines are natural den creatures, thanks to the thousands of years their ancestors spent living in caves and cavities in the ground. Thus pups adapt quite naturally to crate confinement. Puppies are also inherently clean and hate to soil their "dens" or living

Aside from the crate, your pup's lead will be the most important accessory in training him to relieve himself outdoors.

spaces, which makes the crate a natural house-training aid. Thus your dog's crate is actually a multi-purpose dog accessory; it is your Weim's personal dog house within your house, a humane house-training tool, a security measure that will protect your pup as well as your household when you're not home, a travel aid to house and protect your dog when traveling (most motels will accept a crated dog) and, finally, a comfy dog space for your puppy when your anti-dog relatives come to visit.

Outside time usually translates to fun and games. Train your puppy to do his business before racing for his toy.

Some experienced breeders insist on crate use after their puppies leave, and a few even crate-train their pups before they send them home. But it's more likely that your Weim has never seen a crate, so it's up to you to make sure his introduction to it is a pleasant one.

When first introducing your Weimaraner to his crate, toss a tiny treat into the crate to entice him to go

House-training your puppy, beginning as soon as he comes home, is the key to a clean and happy life with your Weim.

in. Continue doing this for the first day or two. Pick a crate command, such as "Kennel," "Inside" or "Crate," and use it when he enters. Introduce the crate as soon as he comes home so he learns that this is his new "house." You also can feed his first few meals inside the crate with the door still open, so the crate association will be a happy one.

Puppy should sleep in his crate from his very first night. He may whine or object to the confinement, but be strong and stay the course. If you release him when he cries, you provide his first life lesson…if I cry, I get out and may be hugged. Hmmm…not a good plan after all—for you.

A better scheme is to place the crate next to your bed at night for the first few weeks. Your presence will comfort him, and you'll also know if he needs a middle-of-the-night potty trip.

Whatever you do, do not lend comfort by taking puppy into bed with you. To a dog, on the bed means equal, which is not a good idea this early on.

Make a practice of placing puppy into his crate for naps, at nighttime and whenever you are unable to watch him closely. Not to worry…he will let you know when he wakes up and needs a potty trip. If he falls asleep under a table and wakes up when you're not there, guess what he'll do first? Make a puddle, then toddle over to say "Hi!"

Become a Weimaraner vigilante. Routines, consistency and an eagle eye are your keys to house-training success. Puppies always "go" when they wake up (quickly now!), after eating, after play periods and after brief periods of confinement. Most pups under 12 weeks of age will need to eliminate at least every hour or so, or up to 10 times a day. (Set your kitchen timer to remind you.) Always take puppy outside to the same area, telling him "Outside" as you go out. Pick a potty word ("Hurry up," "Go potty" and "Get busy" are the most popular) and use it when he does his business, lavishing him with "Good puppy!" praise. Always use the same exit door for these potty trips, and confine puppy to the exit area so he can find it when he needs it. Watch for sniffing and circling, sure signs that he needs to relieve himself. Don't allow him to roam the house until he's house-trained...how will he find that outside door if he's three or four rooms away? He does not have a house map in his head.

Of course, he will have potty accidents. All puppies do. If you catch him in the act, clap your hands, say "No!" loudly and scoop him up to go outside. Your voice should startle him and make him stop. Be sure to praise him when he finishes his duty outside.

If you discover the piddle spot after the fact...more than three or four seconds

By the time your Weim is an adult, the house-training routine will be exactly that: routine.

later...you're too late. All dogs only understand at the moment and will not understand a correction given more than five seconds (that's only *five*) after the deed. Correcting any later will only cause fear, confusion and possible aberrant behavior. Just forget it and vow to be more vigilant.

Never (that is spelled N-E-V-E-R) rub your puppy's nose in his mistake or strike your puppy or adult dog with your hand, a newspaper or other object to correct him, or for any other reason. He will not understand and will only become fearful of the person who is hitting or abusing him.

House-training hint: remove puppy's water after 7 p.m. to aid in nighttime bladder control. If he gets thirsty, offer him an ice cube. Then just watch him race for the refrigerator when he hears the rattle of the ice-cube tray!

Despite its many benefits, crate use can be abused. Puppies under 12 weeks of age should never be confined for more than two hours at a time, unless, of course, they are sleeping. A general rule of thumb is three hours maximum for a three-month-old pup, four hours for a four- to five-month old and no more than six hours for dogs over six months of age. If you're unable to be home to release the dog, arrange for a relative, neighbor or dog-sitter to let him out to exercise and potty.

If you are unable to use a crate for house-training, paper-training does not present a viable option for a Weimaraner. It is not advisable to paper-train your Weim unless you are certain that no paper other than his will ever be on the floor. If you train him to relieve himself on paper, you can hardly reprimand him when he piddles on the Sunday paper left on the living room carpet or a stack of bills inadvertently left on your office floor. The same basic theory applies to chewing. You can't offer your Weim an old slipper to chew on and then scold him for gnawing on your new leather boots. In short, the crate is the best option for house-training your Weimaraner.

What to do with an uncrated puppy when you're not home? Confine him to one area with a dog-proof barrier. Puppy-proofing alone won't be enough protection even in a stripped environment…a bored Weim pup may even chew through drywall. An exercise pen 4 feet by 4 feet square (available through pet suppliers), and sturdy enough that pup can't knock it down, will provide safe containment for short periods. Paper one area for elimination, with perhaps a blanket in the opposite corner for napping. Weim puppies are seldom content to lie around chomping on a chew toy. If you don't or won't crate-train and cannot supervise your pup, be prepared to meet the consequences.

Most importantly, remember that successful house-training revolves around consistency and repetition. Maintain a strict schedule and use your key words consistently. Well-trained owners have well-trained Weimaraner pups.

HOUSE-TRAINING YOUR WEIMARANER

Overview

- The first task that all puppy owners must undertake is housebreaking, teaching the dog clean indoor behavior.
- The crate is the most reliable way to house-train your Weimaraner. Learn how to use a crate properly, never for punishment.
- Teach a "potty" command to use when it's time for puppy to go out to relieve himself.
- Control your puppy's water intake, especially before bedtime.
- Paper training is not a viable option for getting started with your Weimaraner puppy. You will likely want to train your Weim to use a crate and to "go" outdoors.

Teaching Basic Commands

S tart your Weim's puppy lessons as soon as he comes home. Research has proven that the earlier you begin, the easier the process and the more successful you both will be.

Training your Weim to heel makes the difference between enjoyable daily walks and aggravating daily struggles.

COME COMMAND

This command has life-saving potential...preventing your Weim from running into the street, going after a squirrel, chasing a child on a bike...the list goes on and on. Always practice this command on leash. You can't afford to risk failure, or your pup will learn that he does not have to come when called. He needs to learn *always* to come reliably.

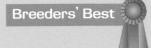

Once you have the pup's attention, call him from a short distance with "Puppy, Come!" (use your happy voice!) and give a treat when he comes to you. If he hesitates, tug him to you gently with his leash. Back up as you draw him to you. Vary the distances so he learns to come to you regardless of how close or far away you are. Grasp and hold his collar with one hand as you dispense the treat. This is important. You will eventually phase out the treat and switch to only hands-on praise. This maneuver also connects holding his collar with coming and treating. Practice for ten minutes twice a day. Keep it fun! Like that of a child, your Weim's attention span is limited. Once he has mastered the come command, continue to practice daily to engrave this most important behavior into his puppy brain. Experienced owners know, however, that you can never completely trust a dog to come when called if the dog is bent on a self-

Your Weim must be reliable with the basic commands in order for you to progress to more advanced activities together.

For the sit/stay, start with the dog sitting by your side before stepping out in front of him. Use a hand signal to reinforce that you want him to stay put.

appointed mission. "Off-leash" is unfortunately often synonymous with "out of control."

SIT COMMAND

This one's a snap, since your Weim already understands the treating process. Stand in front of your pup, move the treat directly over his nose and slowly move it backwards. As he folds backwards to reach the goodie, his rear will move downward to the floor. If the puppy raises up to reach the treat, just lower it a bit. The moment his behind touches the floor, tell him "Sit." (That's one word…"Sit.") Release the treat and gently grasp his collar as you did with "Come." He will again make that positive connection between the treat, the sit position and the collar hold.

As time goes by, make him hold the sit position longer before you treat (this is the beginning of the stay command). You should choose a release word (such as "OK") to use with all commands, signaling to the pup that the exercise is over and he is free to relax. Start using your release word to release him from the sit position. Practice using the sit command for everyday activities, such as sitting for his food bowl or a toy. Do random sits throughout the day, always for a food or praise reward. With every new lesson, your pup is expanding his vocabulary.

STAY COMMAND

"Stay" is really just an extension of "Sit," which your Weim already knows. With puppy sitting when commanded, place the palm of your hand in front of his nose and tell him "Stay." Count to five. Give him his release word to free him from the stay position and then praise. Stretch out the stays in tiny increments…making allowances for puppy energy. Once he stays reliably, take one step backward, then forward again. Gradually extend the time and distance that you move away. If puppy moves from his stay position, say "No" and move forward in front of him. Use sensible timelines depending on your puppy's attention span.

DOWN COMMAND

Down can be a tough command to master. Because the down is a submissive posture, take-charge breeds like the Weim may find it especially difficult. That's why it's most important to teach it when your pup is very young.

From the sit position, move the food lure from his nose to the ground and slightly backward between his front paws. Wiggle it as necessary to spark his interest. As soon as his front legs and rear end hit the floor, give the treat and tell him "Down, good boy, down!",

thus connecting the word to the behavior. Be patient, and be generous with the praise when he cooperates.

Once he goes into the down position with ease,

During your training sessions, your Weim will make a positive association between your holding his collar and staying by your side.

incorporate the stay command as you did with the sit. By six months of age, the puppy should be able to do a solid sit/stay for ten minutes, ditto for a down/stay.

HEEL COMMAND

The actual heel command comes a bit later in the

learning curve. At first, a young Weim should be taught simply to walk politely on a leash, at or near your side. That is best accomplished before your Weim is capable of pulling you down the street.

Start leash training when your pup is ready—no need to rush his education. Simply attach the leash to his buckle collar and let him drag it around for a little while every day. If he chews his leash, distract him with play activities or spray the leash with a product made to deter chewing, which will make it taste unpleasant. Play a game with the leash on.

After a few days, gather up the leash in a distraction-free zone in the house or yard and take just a few steps together. Hold a treat lure at your side to encourage the puppy to walk next to you. Pat your knee and use a happy voice. Move forward just a few steps each time. Say "Let's go!"

when you move forward, hold the treat to keep him near, take a few steps and then give the treat and praise!

Keep these sessions short and happy, a mere 30 seconds at a time. Never scold or nag him into walking faster or slower; just encourage him with happy talk. Walk straight ahead at first, adding wide turns once he gets the hang of it. Progress to 90° turns, using a gentle leash tug, a happy verbal "Let's go!" and, of course, a treat. Walk in short 30- to 40-second bursts, with a happy break (use your release word) and brief play (hugs will do nicely) in between. Keep total training time short and always quit with success, even if just a few short steps.

WAIT COMMAND
You'll love this one, especially when your Weim comes in the house with wet or muddy paws. Work on the wait command with a closed door.

Start to open the door as if to go through or out. When your dog tries to follow, step in front and body-block him to prevent his passage. Don't use the actual wait command just yet. Keep this up until he gives up and you can open the door a little to pass through. Then say "Through" or "Okay" and let him go through the door. Repeat by body-blocking until he understands and waits for you, then start applying the command "Wait" to the behavior. Practice in different doorways inside your home, using outside entrances (to safe or enclosed areas) only after he will wait reliably.

KEEP PRACTICING

Ongoing practice in obedience is actually a lifetime dog rule, especially for a strong-willed Weim. Dogs will be dogs, and, if we don't maintain their skills, they will sink back into sloppy, inattentive behaviors that will be harder to correct. Incorporate these commands into your daily routine and your dog will remain a gentleman of whom you can be proud.

TEACHING BASIC COMMANDS

Overview

- Get started with basic obedience training the right way. Begin when your Weim puppy is young but old enough to accept gentle correction. Choose a quiet (distraction-free) place for lessons and keep lessons short and positive.
- Remember that your Weim will bore easily with too much repetition.
- The basic commands include come, sit, stay, down, heel and wait.
- Practice with your Weimaraner often so that he becomes consistent 100% of the time. Practice should continue throughout the dog's life.
- Your Weimaraner's mastery of commands is essential for his good manners and safety.

CHAPTER 10

Home Care for Your Weimaraner

A quality health-care program is the best gift you can give to your Weim, second only to a loving home. A strong focus on wellness will help keep sickness on the back burner of his life.

Of the regimens included in this chapter, two are, without question, the most important…weight control and dental hygiene.

Hands-on examination helps you tell whether your Weim is at his correct weight, as well as detect any skin or coat abnormalities that are not easily visible.

A HEALTHY WEIGHT

Veterinarians tell us that over 50% of the dogs they see are grossly overweight and that such obesity will take two to three years off a dog's life,

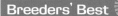

given the strain it puts on the animal's heart, lungs and joints. The obvious message here is that lean is healthier!

To determine whether your Weim is overweight, you should be able to feel your dog's ribs beneath a thin layer of muscle with very gentle pressure on his rib cage. When viewing your dog from above, you should be able to see a definite waistline; from the side, he should have an obvious tuck-up in his abdomen. Yes, your Weim has a waist, defined by his "moderately tucked-up flank" (as per the AKC standard).

Keep a record of his weight from each annual vet visit. A few extra pounds? Adjust his food portions (eliminate those table scraps!), perhaps switch to a "light," "senior" or lower calorie dog-food formula and gradually increase his exercise. Don't start sprinting around the park if your Weim's exercise previously consisted only of walking to the back yard to do his business or running inside to get a

This Weim looks happy to be in fit and trim condition.

The Weimaraner is naturally active and athletic. If your dog is given enough opportunity to exercise, weight control should not be a problem; in fact, very active dogs sometimes need more food.

cookie. Increase his exercise a little bit at a time.

Excessive weight is especially hard on older dogs with creaky joints. A senior Weimaraner who is sedentary will grow out of shape more quickly. Walking and running (slower for old guys) are still the

Brush your Weim's teeth weekly, with products made for dogs, to keep his teeth, gums and mouth healthy.

best workouts for health maintenance. Tailor your dog's exercise to fit his age and physical condition.

YOUR WEIM'S SMILE
The American Veterinary Dental Society states that, by age three,

80% of dogs exhibit signs of gum disease. (Quick, look at your dog's teeth!) Symptoms include yellow and brown build-up of tartar along the gumline, red or inflamed gums and persistent bad breath. If neglected, these conditions will allow bacteria to accumulate in your dog's mouth and enter your dog's bloodstream through those damaged gums, increasing the risk for disease in vital organs such as the heart, liver and kidneys. It's also known that periodontal disease is a major contributor to kidney disease, which is a common cause of death in older dogs…and highly preventable.

Your vet should examine your Weim's teeth and gums during his annual checkup to make sure they are clean and healthy. During the other 364 days of the year, you are your dog's dentist. Brush his teeth daily, or at least twice a week. Use a doggie toothbrush (designed for the contours of a canine's mouth) and use dog toothpaste flavored with chicken, beef or liver. (Minty "human" toothpaste is harmful to dogs.) If your dog resists a toothbrush, try a nappy washcloth or gauze pad wrapped around your finger. Start the brushing process with gentle gum massages when your pup is very young so he will learn to tolerate and even enjoy the process.

ROUTINE CHECKS

Your weekly grooming sessions should include body checks for lumps (cysts, warts and fatty tumors), hot spots and other skin or coat problems. Rub him down with your hands; don't rely on the brush to find abnormalities. While harmless skin lumps are common in older dogs, many can be malignant, and your vet should examine any abnormality. Mole-like black patches or growths on any body part, especially between the toes, require immediate veterinary inspection. Remember, petting and hugging can also turn up little abnormalities.

Be extra-conscious of dry skin, a flaky coat and thinning hair, all signs of thyroid disease. Check for fleas and flea dirt if you think fleas may be present.

Don't forget those two big "E's"—the ears and eyes. Check your Weim's big, velvety ears weekly…are they clean and fresh-smelling? Have your vet show you the proper way to clean them. Remember, too, that many old dogs grow deaf with age. Sure, a smart dog develops selective hearing and sometimes will not "hear" you, but you'll know it's a true hearing deficit when he no longer hears the clinking of the cookie jar. Time and experience will show you what changes and allowances to make if your dog develops hearing loss.

Your Weim's eyes also may deteriorate with age. A bluish haze is common in geriatric dogs and does not impair vision, but you should always check with your vet about *any* changes in the eyes to determine whether it's harmless or indicative of a problem.

How about the other end? Does your dog chew at his rear or scoot and rub it on the carpet? That may be a sign of impacted anal glands or internal parasites. Your vet can show you how to handle either situation.

Have annual stool cultures done to check for internal parasites. Hookworms, whipworms and roundworms

Your Weimaraner will jump for joy over the love and good care that you give him every day.

can cause weight and appetite loss, poor coat quality and all manner of intestinal problems, and can weaken your dog's resistance to other canine diseases. See your vet if any of these signs appear. Tapeworms, common parasites that come from fleas, look like large, flattened grains tucked in the stool.

Heart disease is common in all canines, yet it is a problem that dog owners most frequently overlook. Symptoms include panting and shortness of breath, chronic coughing, especially at night or upon first waking in the morning, and changes in sleeping habits. Heart disease can be treated if you catch it early.

Kidney disease also can be treated successfully with early diagnosis. Dogs seven years of age and older should be tested annually for healthy kidney and liver function. If your dog drinks excessive amounts of water, urinates more frequently or has accidents in the house, run, don't walk, to your vet. Kidney failure can be managed with special diets to reduce the workload on the kidneys.

EMERGENCY CARE

The moral here is…know your Weim. Early detection is the key to your dog's longevity and quality of life. For everyday commonsense care, every dog owner should know the signs of an emergency. Many dog agencies, humane societies and animal shelters sponsor canine first-aid seminars. Participants learn how to recognize and deal with signs of common emergency situations, how to assemble a first-aid kit and how to give CPR to a dog.

Obvious emergencies include vomiting for more than 24 hours, bloody or prolonged (over 24 hours) diarrhea, fever (normal canine temperature is 101.5°F), a sudden swelling of any body part, especially near the nose and throat (allergic reaction to an insect bite or other stimulus) or any symptoms of bloat, which require immediate veterinary care.

Keep a detailed list of situations and symptoms handy. Again, know your dog so that you'll be able to recognize changes that could indicate a problem. Your Weim's life could depend on it.

HOME CARE FOR YOUR WEIMARANER

Overview

- Weight control and dental care should be priorities in every Weim owner's home-care routine. Obesity can shorten the life of your Weimaraner, as can plaque accumulation and the diseases associated with it.
- During weekly grooming sessions, keep an eye on the condition of your Weim's coat. Always watch for moles, bumps, lumps and parasites, all of which can lead to serious problems.
- Know the signs of wellness, symptoms of illness and first-aid techniques so you can recognize a problem and act responsibly.

WEIMARANER

Feeding Your Weimaraner

A polite Weim won't beg for "people food," and a smart Weim knows that it's not good for him anyway!

Feeding your dog is like putting gasoline into your car. You can't use a poor-quality product and expect maximum performance or results. A quality dog food is the best route to your Weimaraner's overall health. The less expensive foods do not provide a fully digestible product, nor do they contain a proper balance of the vitamins, minerals and fatty acids that are necessary to support healthy muscle, tissue, skin and coat. Consult your breeder or vet for the best guidance about feeding your Weimaraner. The price of the food is not a fool-proof guide. Learn to read the label.

Premium dog-food manufacturers have developed their formulas with strict quality controls, using only quality ingredients obtained from reliable sources. The labels on the food bags tell you what ingredients are in the food (beef, chicken, corn, etc.), with the ingredients listed in descending order of weight or amount in the food. Do not add your own supplements, "people food" or extra vitamins to the food. You will only upset the nutritional balance of the dog food, which could negatively affect the growth pattern of your Weimaraner pup and/or healthy maintenance of your adult dog.

The best nutrition for pups in their first weeks of life is their mother's milk. Once weaned, it's the breeder's responsibility to start them off on a quality puppy food to promote healthy growth.

In the world of quality dog foods, there are enough choices to confuse even experienced dog folks. The major dog-food manufacturers now offer formulas for every size, age

Water is an essential part of any dog's diet. Adults should have access to clean fresh water 24 hours a day.

and activity level. The new "growth" foods contain protein and fat levels that are appropriate for the different-sized breeds. Fast-growing breeds like the Weimaraner require less protein and fat during their early months of rapid growth, which is better for healthy joint development. Accordingly, medium and small breeds also have different nutritional requirements during their first year of growth. Ask your breeder and your vet what food they recommend for your Weim puppy.

As with human infants, puppies require a diet different from that of an adult. If you plan to switch from the food fed by your breeder, take home a small supply of the breeder's food to mix with your own to aid your puppy's adjustment to his new food.

When and how much to feed? An eight-week-old puppy does best eating three times a day. (Tiny tummies, tiny meals.) At about 12 weeks of age, you can switch to twice-daily feeding. Most breeders suggest two meals a day for the life of the dog, regardless of the breed of dog.

Although the cause of bloat is unknown, many breeders still offer many observations. There are no guarantees. Smaller meals, rather than one large daily feeding, may help prevent the possibility of bloat, as some theories suggest that gulping large amounts of food or drinking copious amounts of water right after eating can contribute to the condition. Other potentially helpful measures include no heavy exercise for at least an hour before eating and two hours afterward. Make sure your dog is not overly excited during meals.

Free feeding is not

recommended. Free feeding fosters picky eating habits...a bite here, a nibble there. Free feeders also are more likely to become

come from you, his owner.

With scheduled meals, it's also easier to predict elimination, which is the better road to house-

Discuss the use of elevated bowl stands with your vet, as there is a debate about whether or not they're helpful.

possessive of their food bowls, a problem behavior that signals the beginning of resource-guarding and aggression. Scheduled meals give you one more opportunity to remind your Weim that all good things in life

training. Regular meals help you know just how much puppy eats and when, valuable information so you can recognize changes in his appetite and thus recognize when he is not feeling well.

Weimaraner

Like people, puppies and adult dogs have different appetites; some will eat, lick their food bowls clean and beg for more, while others pick at their food and leave some of it untouched. It's easy to overfeed a chow hound. Who can resist those pleading Weimaraner eyes? Be strong and stay the right course. Chubby puppies may be cute and cuddly, but the extra weight will stress their growing joints and is thought to be a factor in the development of hip and elbow disease. Overweight pups also tend to grow into overweight adults who tire easily and will be more susceptible to other health problems.

So always remember that the best weight for your dog is whatever is appropriate to his height and bone. Quite simply, a leaner dog is likely to be healthier than an obese dog. And that doesn't even reflect the better quality of life for the lean dog that can run, jump and play without the burden of an extra 10 or 20 pounds.

Dry food is recommended by most vets, since the dry particles help clean the dog's teeth of plaque and tartar. A carrot now and then is a healthy treat with dental benefits. Adding water to dry food is optional. The food hog who almost inhales his food will do better with a splash of water in his food bowl. A bit of water added immediately before eating is also thought to enhance the flavor of the food while still preserving the dental benefits. Whether feeding wet or dry, always have water available at all times.

To complicate the dog-food dilemma, there are also raw foods available for those who prefer to feed their dogs a completely natural diet rather than traditional manufactured dog food. The debate about raw and/or all-natural vs. manufactured is a fierce one, with the raw-food proponents claiming that raw diets have cured their dogs' allergies and other chronic ailments. If you are interested in this alternative feeding method, there are several books on raw diets written by nutrition experts. You can also check with your vet, ask your breeder and surf the Internet.

If your adult dog is overweight, you can switch to a "light" food that has fewer calories and more fiber. "Senior" foods for older dogs have formulas designed to meet the needs of older, less active dogs. "Performance" diets contain more fat and protein for dogs that compete in sporting disciplines or lead very active lives. The bottom line is this: what and how much you feed your dog are major factors in his overall health and longevity. It's worth your investment in extra time to provide the best diet for your dog. You are best advised to check with your vet.

FEEDING YOUR WEIMARANER

Overview

- Offering a top-quality dog food is the most reliable and convenient way to provide complete nutrition for your Weimaraner.
- Discuss with your vet and/or breeder the best type of food, amounts and the feeding schedule for your Weim.
- Avoid free feeding.
- Learn to read the dog-food labels and to understand what they indicate for your dog's diet.
- Your Weimaraner's good health depends largely upon a proper diet.

Grooming Your Weimaraner

Weimaraners are considered easy keepers with short coats that require minimal care. However, grooming involves more than just brushing your dog. It also includes his ears, teeth and nails, and thorough body checks for external parasites, lumps and bumps. Good grooming habits are an essential part of your Weim's health-care program and should be a weekly routine all year long.

Every dog should enjoy the hands-on grooming process; it's the next

After your Weim puppy has been lounging on the lawn, be sure to check his coat for visitors (aka fleas and ticks).

best thing to petting. To that end, the brush, nail clippers and toothbrush are best introduced when your Weim is just a pup. Some older dogs who have not experienced these ministrations may object when they are older…and bigger…and better able to resist. Grooming will then become a distasteful chore, even a battle, rather than a routine procedure that both of you can enjoy.

The short, close coat of the Weimaraner does not need complicated grooming, only regular attention, to look its sleek, shiny best.

Hold your first grooming session as soon as your puppy has adjusted to his new home base. Start with tiny increments of time, stroking him gently with a soft brush, briefly handling his paws, looking inside his ears, gently touching his gums. Offer little bits of dog treats during each session so that he'll think such personal contact is a prelude to a feast. Ah, the power of positive association.

The Weimaraner coat is short, glossy and virtually groom-free.

Too-frequent bathing is not advised, as it can dry out the skin and coat. However, the need will arise should your Weim get his paws into something dirty.

His coat is dander-free and not highly allergenic, which makes the Weim a good choice for people who are allergic to dog dander. His short coat requires little more than a weekly brushing with a soft bristle brush to remove dust, stimulate circulation and distribute oils in the skin. During shedding season, brushing outdoors with a Shed'n blade or rubber curry works very well.

Frequent bathing is not necessary, and, in fact, will remove the essential oils that keep your dog's skin supple, his coat soft and gleaming. Of course, there are those times when a bath is necessary. The bathing process can be a challenge if your Weim dislikes water or getting lathered up.

To minimize the stress and struggle of bath time, start when your pup is small. Imagine wrestling a full-grown adult into the tub or shower stall. Lure your puppy into the tub with the usual food rewards, perhaps enhancing them with tasty stuff like squirt cheese or peanut butter to make bath time extra-appealing. Line the tub or shower with a towel or rubber mat for safe footing. Start with a dry tub and, after pup is comfortable there, gradually add shallow water and then bathe him. He may never learn to love it, but all you need is his cooperation.

When bathing him, always be sure to rinse the coat completely to avoid any

Longhaired Weimaraners will require a little more grooming than the shorthaired variety, paying special attention to the areas of feathering so that no matting occurs.

itching from residual shampoo. A good chamois is ideal for drying, as it absorbs water like a sponge. Keep him away from drafts for a good while after bathing and drying to prevent chilling.

process, so start nail clipping as soon as possible, since the longer you wait, the less he will cooperate. Try to make it a positive experience so that he at least tolerates it without a major battle. Offer those

Dogs can't always reach to scratch an itch! All dogs scratch from time to time, but frequent scratching can indicate a problem and is a signal to visit the vet.

Nails should be trimmed as needed. This is always the least favorite grooming chore, and the one most often neglected. Puppies naturally do not like the nail-clipping

puppy treats with each clipping session. Thus the puppy will learn that when you touch his paws or trim those nails, he will receive a food reward.

At first you may have to settle on only one or two nails at a time to avoid a wrestling match. It is better to trim a small amount of nail more frequently than trying to cut back a nail that has grown too long. Nip off the nail tip or clip at the curved part of the nail. Be careful not to cut the quick (the pink vein in the nail), as that is quite painful, and the nail may bleed profusely. You can stanch the bleeding with a few drops of a clotting solution available from your veterinarian or drug store (where it is sold for shaving cuts). Keep it on hand… accidents happen.

Weekly ear checks are worth the proverbial pound of cure. Ear infections are common to all breeds of dog, with some Weims more prone to chronic ear infection than others. The Weimaraner's long drop ears can act like a terrarium cover that prevents air flow and keeps the ear canal moist and ripe for musty growths, especially in humid climates. Regular cleansing, especially after swimming, with a specially formulated ear cleanser will keep your dog's ears clean and odor-free.

Symptoms of ear infection include redness and/or swelling of the ear flap or inner ear, a nasty odor or a dark, waxy discharge. If your

Accustoming your Weim to having his nails clipped as a puppy means you won't have to struggle with an adult who objects to his pedicures.

dog digs at his ear(s) with his paw, shakes his head a lot or appears to lose his balance, see your vet at once.

The two most common mistakes that owners make when dealing with an ear infection are waiting too long to seek treatment and failing to treat the ear during the entire course of medication, which allows the infection to smolder and

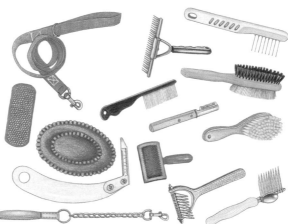

You'll find quite an array of doggie accessories and grooming tools out there, but you'll only need a few basic items for your Weim's grooming routine.

sprout up again. Be proactive with your Weimaraner's ear care and the better he'll hear you say "I love you!"

GROOMING YOUR WEIMARANER

Overview

- While the Weimaraner is easy to groom, proper coat care is a vital part of his overall maintenance program for good health and must be initiated when the pup is young.
- The Weim owner also must tend to his dog's nails and ears.
- You will only have to bathe your Weimaraner occasionally, probably only a few times per year unless he gets into something dirty.
- When dealing with ear problems, owners must not wait too long to seek treatment and always must follow through with the medication for its entire prescribed course.

Keeping Your Dog Active

Simply stated, the Weimaraner needs to exercise. More than just an outlet for gundog energy, physical activity is fundamental to your Weimaraner's mental health and stability. Without it, he will become bored and creatively destructive. Although all canines benefit from some form of daily exercise, the Weimaraner needs something to keep his body and his mind occupied.

That said, bear in mind that neither the Weimaraner puppy nor adult will get proper exercise on his own. He needs a reason or incentive

Your Weim certainly has the ability to leap and jump about, but don't encourage this kind of activity while the puppy is still growing and developing.

to keep moving, and that incentive is, of necessity, the person in charge of his life. A long, brisk daily walk or, better yet, two walks a day, will help keep your adult Weimaraner fit and trim, as well as keeping his mind stimulated with the sights and sounds of the neighborhood. How long and how far to walk depends on your dog's age and physical condition, although most Weims have great endurance and can probably outwalk their owners.

A young Weimaraner's bones are relatively soft, and his growth plates do not fully close until at least about 14 months of age. Thus his musculoskeletal structure is more vulnerable to injury during that growth period and should not be subjected to heavy stress. That means shorter walks at more frequent intervals for the youngster and no games that encourage twisting, high jumping or heavy impact on his front

Agility trials offer Weimaraner and owner a challenging and exciting outlet for their talents and training.

Conformation showing is perhaps the most popular type of canine competition.

or rear. Playtime with other puppies and older dogs also should be supervised to avoid excessive wrestling and twisting until your pup is past the danger age. Swimming, whenever possible, is excellent low-impact exercise.

The Weimaraner demonstrates his athletic and effortless gait in the show ring.

When and where to walk is as important as how long. On warm days, avoid walking during midday heat and go out during the cooler morning or evening hours. If you're a jogger, your Weimaraner is the perfect running companion. Just make sure that your buddy is fully developed, in good condition and up to doing your mile-plus run.

Your daily walks are also excellent bonding sessions. Your Weim will look forward eagerly to his special one-on-one time with you. As a creature of habit, your dog will bounce with joy when he sees you don your cap, pick up his leash or rattle your keys.

Walks alone, however, are not enough. Your Weimaraner needs to be busy, doing things with his favorite person—you, of course! Take your exercise program to another level by planning a weekly night out with your Weim and enrolling in a class. The benefits of obedience class are endless. You will be motivated to work with your dog daily at home so you don't look unprepared at each week's class. Your dog will have a grand old time, and so will you. You'll both be more active and thus healthier. Your dog will learn the basics of obedience, will be better behaved and will become a model canine citizen. He will discover that you really are the boss, and you will assume the throne as the king of his dog world. Sound good?

Agility class offers even more healthy outlets for the adult Weimaraner's energy. He will learn to scale an A-frame ramp, race headlong through a tunnel, balance himself on a teeter-totter, jump onto and off a platform, jump through hoops and run between a line of posts. The challenge of learning to navigate these agility obstacles, and his success in mastering each one, will make you both proud.

Be sure to keep beginning heights very low and make sure the work surfaces are made of a resilient material to limit impact on those growing bones and muscles.

Regardless, you cannot start training your Weim in agility until he is at least one year of age, once his bones and ligaments have grown strong enough to support his heavy body. Gawky adolescents should never be balancing on a dog walk!

Agility trials are fun for dog, owner and spectator. Weims tackle the agility obstacles, ike the tire jump, with grace and enthusiasm.

Weimaraner

You can take your activities one step further and participate with your dog in obedience and agility competition. Trials are held year-round and are designed for all levels of experience. Find a club or join a training group. Working with other fanciers will give you the incentive to keep working with your

As an HPR breed, your Weim can certainly be trained to retrieve from the water. Even if you don't do water retrieving with your dog, he will likely enjoy an occasional swim in safe waters.

licensed pointing trials that are designed for the hunt-point-retrieve (HPR) breeds. In many of the stakes, the dogs are teamed with handlers on horseback. However, the WCA also requires that dogs retrieve as well as point. In order to become a Weimaraner field champion, a dog must earn four points in shoot-to-retrieve stakes as well as pass a water retrieving test. The WCA also uses a series of hunting ratings to evaluate each dog.

If you hope to hunt with your Weimaraner or compete in field events, it's important to start training early to develop good habits and channel his instincts in the right direction. Even if your Weim is primarily a pet,

dog. Check the Weimaraner Club of America and AKC websites for details and contact people.

The Weimaraner is also eligible to compete in AKC-

you will both benefit immensely from the discipline involved in field training as you would from obedience work. Read up on fundamental training methods and speak to experienced trainers before you begin; consider enlisting the help of a trainer. Contact WCA officers for more information on field training and events like hunt tests and field trials.

Conformation is by far the most popular canine competition for all breeds.

If you plan to show your Weimaraner, make sure you start with a show-quality puppy and discuss your goals with the breeder. Most local breed clubs host show-training classes and can help a novice get started with his pup. As with other competitions, it's best to start when your Weim is young so he develops a good ring attitude. It's the only "attitude" that should be encouraged in the Weimaraner.

KEEPING YOUR DOG ACTIVE

Overview

- Allow your Weimaraner daily on-lead walks along with free running time in a safely enclosed area.
- Do not let puppies exert themselves, as they are more prone to injury when young. Do not overdo exercise on warm days, puppy or adult.
- Daily walks reinforce that special bond between you and your Weim.
- Additionally, consider enrolling in an obedience class to give you and your Weimaraner another fun outlet together.
- Conformation shows and obedience and agility trials are excellent forums for dog and owner.
- You can develop your Weim's innate abilities with field training and trials.

WEIMARANER

Your Weimaraner and His Vet

When you choose your veterinarian, you're selecting your Weimaraner's HMO. This is an important decision that will bind the three of you in sickness and in health. Check with local breed clubs, friends and co-workers to find a qualified veterinarian you can trust. You can also check with the American Association of Veterinary State Boards (www.aavsb.org/dir.asp) to find out if any complaints have been lodged against a vet you are considering.

Take your puppy to your veteri-

Your puppy should have the proper vaccinations before you take him out and about around other dogs. Many diseases are easily transmitted from dog to dog, and an unvaccinated pup is vulnerable.

narian of choice within three or four days of bringing him home. Show the vet any health records of shots and wormings from your breeder. The vet should conduct a thorough physical exam to make sure your Weimaraner is in good health, determine what additional booster shots your puppy needs and schedule times to give them. A good vet will be gentle and affectionate with your new pup and do everything possible to make sure that the puppy is neither frightened nor intimidated.

Your vet will manage all aspects of your pup's vaccination schedule, including which vaccinations he gets and how frequently, and the booster-shot program.

Vaccine protocol varies with many veterinarians, but most recommend a series of three "combination" shots given at three- to four-week intervals. Your puppy most likely had his first shot before he left his breeder.

"Combination" shots vary, and a single injection may contain five, six, seven or even eight vaccines in one shot. Many breeders and veterinarians feel the potency in high-combination

Your Weimaraner's health depends on your ability to recognize signs of wellness and signs of potential problems.

vaccines can negatively impact a puppy's immature immune system, so they recommend the lower combinations or even separate vaccines.

Some Weimaraner breeders have found that Weim puppies have a serious allergic reaction to the second and third shots in the puppy series. They recommend separating the distemper and parvo vaccines into single shots and giving them three to four weeks apart. The wisest and most conservative course is to administer only one shot

Meet dog enemy number one—the flea! This greatly enlarged illustration gives an up-close-and-personal view of the peskiest of your pet's pests.

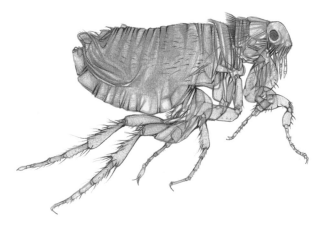

in a single visit, rather than two or three shots at the same time. That means extra trips to your veterinarian with your puppy and adult dog, but your Weim's healthy immune system is worth your time.

VACCINES

The vaccines most commonly recommended by the American Veterinary Medical Association (AVMA) are those that protect against diseases most dangerous to your puppy and adult dog. These include distemper (canine distemper virus—CDV), fatal in puppies; canine parvovirus (CPV or parvo), highly contagious and also fatal in puppies and at-risk dogs; canine adenovirus (CAV2), highly contagious and high-risk for pups under 16 weeks of age; canine hepatitis (CA1), highly contagious for pups at high risk; and rabies, which can be fatal. Rabies immunization is required in all 50 states.

Vaccines no longer routinely recommended by the AVMA, except when the risk is present, are for canine parainfluenza, leptospirosis, canine coronavirus, bordetella (canine cough) and Lyme disease (borreliosis). These diseases are considered neither fatal nor high-risk everywhere. Your veterinarian will alert you if there is an incidence of these diseases in your town or neighborhood so you can immunize accordingly.

HEARTWORM

This is a parasite, a worm that propagates inside your dog's heart and will ultimately kill your dog. Now found in all 50 states, heartworm is delivered through a mosquito bite. Even indoor dogs should take a heartworm preventive, which can be given daily or monthly in pill form, or in a shot given every six months. Heartworm preventatives are prescription medications available only through your veterinarian.

FLEAS AND TICKS

Fleas have been around as long as dogs have, and it's likely that you will battle fleas sometime during your Weimaraner's lifetime. Fortunately, today there are several effective low-toxic flea weapons to aid you in your flea war. Find out from your vet which products he recommends.

Persistent scratching can be indicative of fleas, ticks or other nasty parasites that like to make their homes on unsuspecting dogs.

Lyme disease (canine borreliosis), ehrlichiosis and Rocky Mountain spotted fever are tick-borne diseases now found in almost every state. These diseases are considered neither fatal nor high risk in most places today.

MODERN-DAY HEALTH CONCERNS

A well-informed dog owner is better prepared to raise a healthy dog. Always ask your vet which shots or medications your dog is getting at each visit and what they are for. Keep a notebook or dog diary and record all health information so you won't forget it. Believe me, you can easily forget it if you don't.

Fortunately, today's veterinary community is focused on preventive care and canine wellness as well as treating animals after they are sick. The American Holistic Veterinary Medical Association and other specialty groups now offer acupuncture, herbal remedies, homeopathy and other alternative therapies in addition to traditional disease treatment and prevention. Many pet owners today incorporate both philosophies into their dogs' health-care programs.

Even the annual vaccination protocols that have been standard practice currently are being scrutinized and researched. Many veterinary colleges across the country now recommend vaccinating every three years instead of annually. Research suggests that annual vaccinations may actually be over-vaccinating and contributing to many of today's canine health problems. Many dog owners now have titer tests done to check their dogs' antibodies rather than automatically vaccinating for parvo or distemper.

Rabies vaccination is mandatory in all 50 states.

However, for many years the rabies vaccine has been available in a one-year and a three-year shot. Same protection, so why vaccinate every year?

Regardless of vaccine frequency, every Weimaraner should visit his veterinarian once a year. At the very least, he needs an annual heartworm test before he can receive another year of medication. Most importantly, annual visits keep your vet apprised of your pet's health progress, and the hands-on exams often turn up small abnormalities that you can't see or feel.

Your Weim's health is in your hands between those annual visits to the vet. Be ever-conscious of any changes in his appearance or behavior. Here are some things to consider:

Has your Weimaraner gained a few too many pounds or suddenly lost weight? Are his teeth clean and white? Is he urinating more frequently, drinking more water than usual? Does he strain during a bowel movement? Any changes in his appetite? Does he appear short of breath, lethargic, overly tired? Have you noticed limping or any sign

Beautiful, healthy pups with a promising future! Owners should continue their breeders' efforts by developing good relationships with their vets and being diligent about health care at all stages of their Weims' lives.

of joint stiffness? Any or all of these signs signal that a visit to the vet is indicated. This is especially important for the senior dog, since even subtle changes can be a sign of something serious.

SPAYING/NEUTERING

This is almost a non-issue, since to spay or neuter is the best health insurance policy you can give your Weimaraner. Between heats may be the best time to have a bitch spayed. Several cancers can be avoided by spaying the bitch. Males neutered before their male hormones kick in, usually before six months of age, enjoy zero to greatly reduced risk of testicular and prostate cancer and other related tumors and infections. Additionally, males will be less likely to roam, become aggressive or display those overt male behaviors that drive most people nuts. Statistically, you will make a positive contribution to reducing pet overpopulation and to your dog's long-term health. The bottom line here is: if your Weim is a pet only and will not be shown or bred, to spay or neuter is the thing to do! Consult your vet for the optimum time for neutering or spaying.

YOUR WEIM AND HIS VET

Overview

- Upon bringing your Weim home, take him to the vet for an exam.
- Discuss a vaccination schedule with your vet.
- Heartworm threatens the lives of dogs, though it can be prevented through a prescription drug.
- Parasites like ticks and fleas can lead to various diseases that must be guarded against.
- Keep a close eye on your Weimaraner's behavior and overall condition for signs of potential problems. Knowing your dog's normal behavior makes it easy to recognize a potential problem.
- Spaying/neutering offers many health benefits for pet males and females of any breed.